Language Arts Explorer

NUCLEAR POWER

by Shirley Duke

ENERGY LAB: NUCLEAR POWER

CHERRY LAKE PUBLISHING • ANN ARBOR, MICHIGAN

Published in the United States of America
by Cherry Lake Publishing
Ann Arbor, Michigan
www.cherrylakepublishing.com

Printed in the United States of America
Corporate Graphics Inc.
January 2013
CLFA10

Consultants: Mikael Nilsson, Assistant Professor Department of Chemical Engineering and Materials Science, University of California–Irvine; Marla Conn, reading/literacy specialist and educational consultant

Editorial direction:
Lauren Coss

Book design and illustration:
Christa Schneider

Photo credits: Michael Utech/iStockphoto, cover, 1; Shutterstock Images, 5, 13, 17, 19, 27; iStockphoto, 7; Andrea Danti/Shutterstock Images, 9; Anglian Art/Shutterstock Images, 11; Laura Rauch/AP Images, 15; Iryna Rasko/iStockphoto, 21; A.L. Spangler/Shutterstock Images, 22; Takayuki Hamai/The Yomiuri Shimbun/AP Images, 25

Library of Congress Cataloging-in-Publication Data
Duke, Shirley Smith
Nuclear power / Shirley Duke.
pages cm. – (Energy Lab)
Includes bibliographical references and index.
ISBN 978-1-61080-896-5 (hardback : alk. paper) – ISBN 978-1-61080-921-4 (paperback : alk. paper) – ISBN 978-1-61080-946-7 (ebook) – ISBN 978-1-61080-971-9 (hosted ebook)
1. Nuclear energy–Juvenile literature. I. Title.

TK9148.D78 2013
621.48'3–dc23

2012032788

Cherry Lake Publishing would like to acknowledge the work of The Partnership for 21st Century Skills. Please visit www.21stCenturySkills.org for more information.

TABLE OF CONTENTS

You are being given a mission. The facts in What You Know will help you accomplish it. Remember the clues from What You Know while you are reading the story. The clues and the story will help you answer the questions at the end of the book. Have fun on this adventure!

YOUR MISSION

Your mission is to learn about nuclear power as an energy source. How does it work? Is it safe? Is it better for the environment than other energy sources? Can it be improved? What role might it play in our future energy use? Review the facts in What You Know. Then start your mission to discover more about nuclear power.

WHAT YOU KNOW

- More than 80 percent of our energy comes from **fossil fuels**, including oil, coal, and natural gas.
- Fossil fuels are **nonrenewable**. They also give off a lot of **carbon dioxide** and other types of pollution.
- Scientists want to find ways of producing energy that are more efficient, less expensive, and better for the environment than our current energy sources.
- Nuclear power provides 13.5 percent of the world's electricity. Soon it may be even more common.
- Nuclear power plants produce much less carbon dioxide than fossil fuel power plants. But nuclear power plants

Nuclear power plants produce one-fifth of the electricity used in the United States.

create dangerous radioactive waste that must be stored and protected.

Madison Spencer is learning about nuclear energy by interviewing different experts. She wants to find out how nuclear energy works and how it might be used in the future. Carry out your mission by reading her journal.

March 13:
THE POWER OF THE ATOM

Nuclear energy seems pretty complicated. I've decided to start my research by learning the basics of nuclear power. Ms. Kishi is my older brother's chemistry teacher. I'm hoping she can help with my research.

Ms. Kishi holds up a small foam ball with smaller foam balls suspended around it. "This is a model of an **atom**," she says. "Believe it or not, everything on Earth is made of atoms. Atoms are super tiny. They are much too small for the human eye to see. Atoms have a **nucleus** in the center. This nucleus is made of protons that have a positive charge and neutrons that have no charge. Tiny electrons move around the nucleus. These electrons hold a negative charge. The positive and negative charges balance each other out."

Ms. Kishi explains that the number of protons in an atom decides the type of element that atom is. Two protons make helium. Six protons form carbon. **Uranium** has 92 protons.

"Research in the late 1890s showed energy rays coming from uranium and a few other elements," she says. "Scientists called this energy **radiation**."

"Do the energy particles just shoot off the uranium?" I ask.

Atoms are in everything. Atoms of different elements combine to form molecules. A water molecule is a combination of hydrogen and oxygen atoms.

"Nope, it's a little more complicated than that," Ms. Kishi says. "Basically, we need to split up the uranium atom. When a uranium atom splits, it throws off particles. These particles hit other atoms and cause those atoms to split. This process is known as a chain reaction. Imagine a line of dominoes. When one domino falls, it causes the next one to fall. This is also a chain reaction."

Ms. Kishi explains that splitting a nucleus releases a huge amount of energy. This splitting is called nuclear **fission**. It happens naturally in a few elements, such as uranium and plutonium. During World War II (1939–1945), scientists used nuclear fission to create an atomic bomb.

NUCLEAR RESEARCH

In 1934, Italian American physicist Enrico Fermi experimented with splitting uranium into smaller elements that weighed less. In the 1930s, German chemists Otto Hahn and Fritz Strassmann and Austrian physicist Lise Meitner did similar experiments. The scientists added up the masses of all the elements after fission occurred. But they found that something was missing. The total mass didn't equal the original uranium's total weight. Lise Meitner showed that the missing mass had been changed to energy. Fermi and other scientists later created the first nuclear reactor.

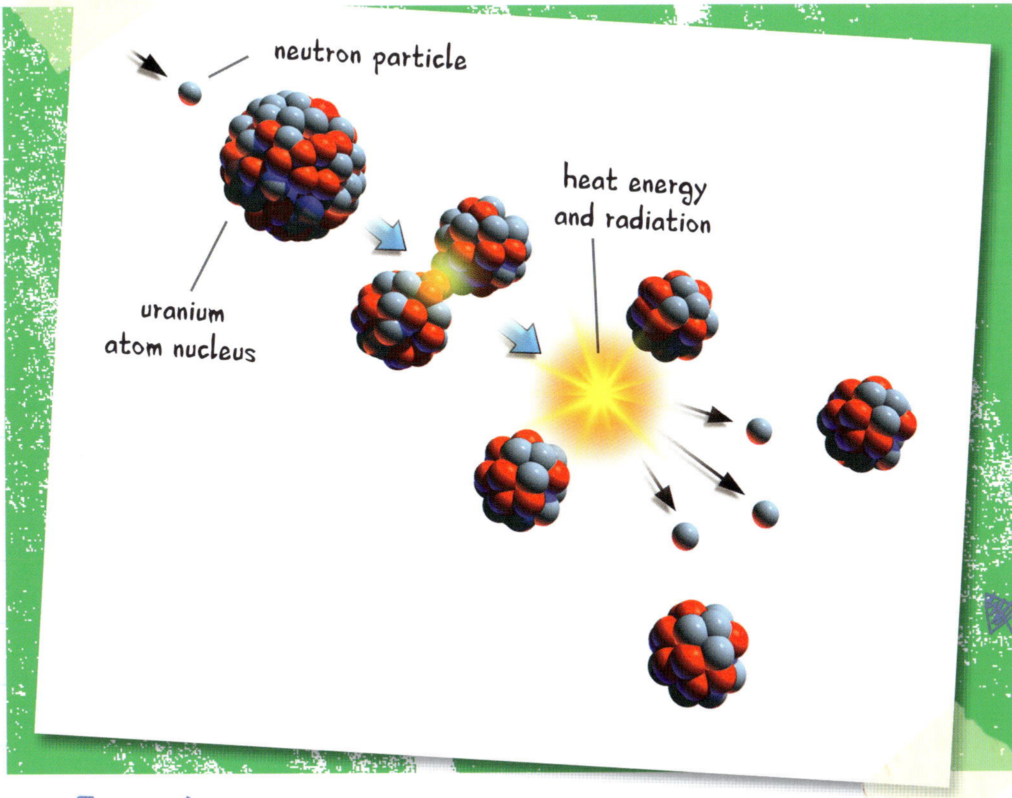

Fission happens when an atom splits. Particles from the split atom can cause other atoms to split, creating a chain reaction.

"After the war, people tried to find peaceful ways to use nuclear energy," she adds. "Such massive amounts of energy could be very useful."

"That led to nuclear power plants," I say.

"Right!" Ms. Kishi says.

Ms. Kishi has helped me learn a lot about the history of nuclear energy. But I want to learn more about nuclear fission. I know where my next stop needs to be. ★

March 20:
NUCLEAR POWER PLANT

I want to learn more about how nuclear power is created. Today, I'm meeting nuclear engineer Bob Young in the lobby of the Northern Waters power-generating facility in River City, Minnesota. Bob explains the actual nuclear power plant is off-limits. But he'll still fill me in on how a nuclear reactor works.

"Did you see the large, rounded dome on the way in?" Bob asks. "That's the containment vessel. It holds the nuclear fuel. The cooling tower lets off the huge, white cloud you saw as you were walking in."

Bob tells me Northern Waters has two reactors. Inside each reactor, uranium fuel in the **core** splits apart into smaller atoms. This causes a chain reaction, just as Ms. Kishi explained. The chain reaction in the fuel releases heat energy. Even though this process releases large amounts of heat, nothing burns.

I tell Bob about Ms. Kishi's dominoes example.

Bob smiles. "Very good! Here's another example. Imagine a box of 100 set mousetraps. If you dropped in one more set trap, the motion of it hitting the other traps would set off that trap. That motion would trigger the next trap to go off, and so on. That would be a chain reaction. If you

One nuclear plant can produce enough power to equal the energy produced by 1,200 windmills.

compare this to nuclear fission, the fuel has run out when the last trap is sprung."

Bob tells me the power plant's core is made of uranium fuel pellets. These pellets are very small. But they hold large amounts of energy. Just one pellet of uranium equals the energy from 150 gallons (568 L) of oil. These pellets are stacked inside 12-foot (4-m) metal rods, which are bundled together. The pellets and rods are called the fuel assembly. Reactors hold many fuel assemblies.

Bob points at a pipe in the model. He explains that the reactors at the Northern Waters plant are pressurized

RADIATION FOR MEDICINE

Radioactive materials aren't just used to generate electricity. Radioactivity is used to find and destroy certain types of cancer cells. However, it can also damage normal cells. This means cancer treatments must be planned carefully. Doctors use other forms of radioactive materials as markers. If a patient has a medical condition a doctor wants to study, the doctor may inject the patient with a weak radioactive marker. Doctors follow the path the markers take to learn how organs or other body parts are working.

water reactors (PWRs). The core of each reactor sits in water. The water flows through the core to heat tubes in a steam generator. The tubes cause water in a separate container to boil and turn into steam. The steam powers a **turbine**, which runs generators to create electricity.

Bob continues, "A condenser catches all the steam. Water from the cooling tower is circulated in the condenser. Then the steam is cooled until it changes back into water. The water can be used again."

Bob says the whole system is pretty environmentally friendly. Just one fuel pellet can create a lot of energy. Nuclear power generating plants give off much less pollution than plants powered by coal.

But if nuclear energy is cleaner, I wonder, why don't we use it more as a power source? ★

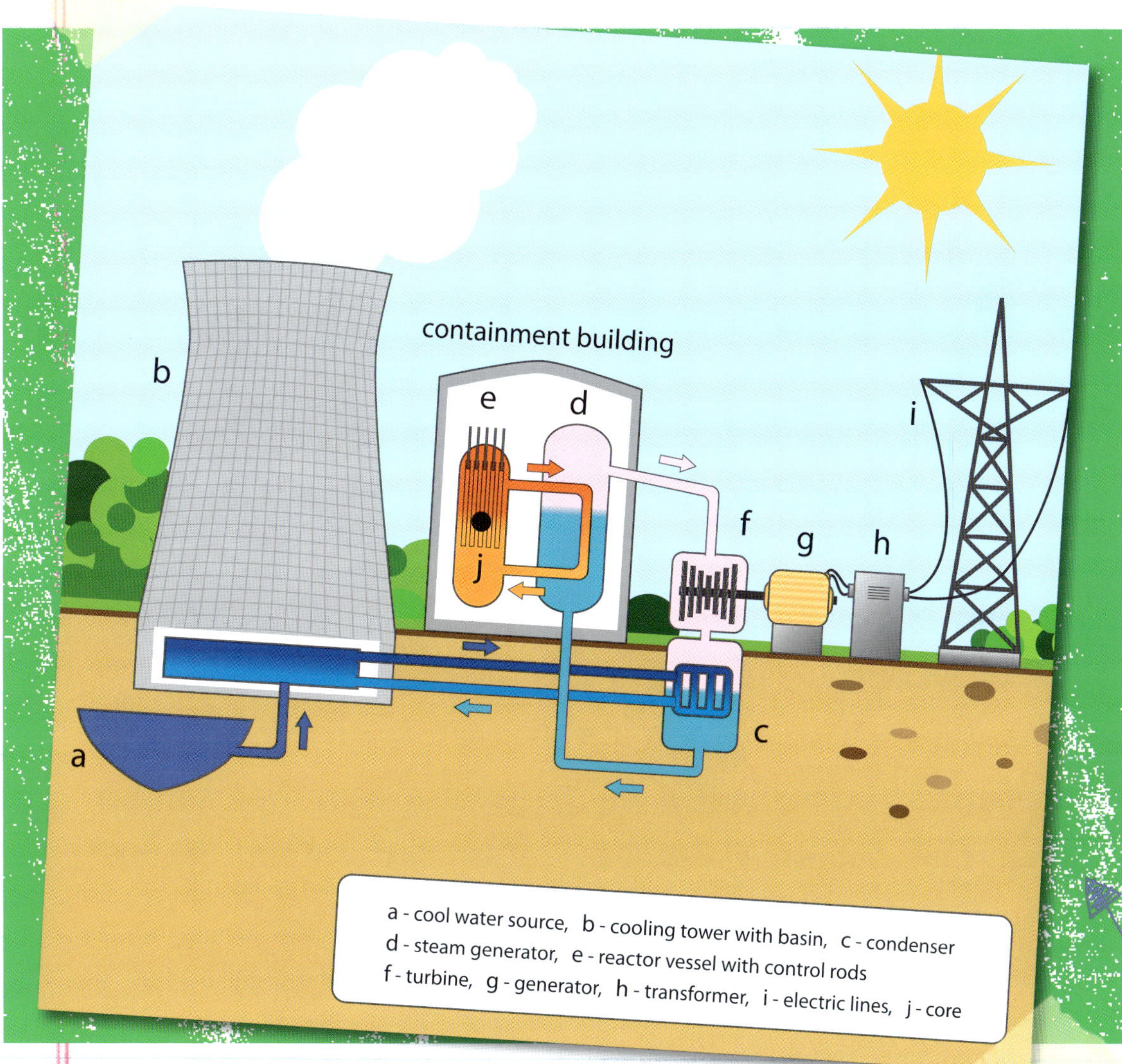

In nuclear power plants, steam turns a turbine to generate electricity.

March 25:
YUCCA MOUNTAIN, NEVADA

Today, I've traveled all the way to Nevada to learn about storing nuclear waste. I can't actually go into the Yucca Mountain nuclear waste storage site. Instead geologist Ted Cruz is driving me near the site so I can view it from afar.

As we drive, Ted gives me some background information on nuclear waste and storage. He reminds me that uranium atoms give off radiation. This means they are decaying. In time, the uranium will decay enough to become a different element. It will be less radioactive

"We measure the decay using the term half-life," Ted explains. "A half-life measures the time it takes for an element to reach the halfway point in its decay. Uranium decays slowly. It can take as long as 4.5 billion years for half of any sample amount to break down into a new element. This means that nuclear waste is still radioactive. Right now, nuclear waste is stored on-site at each reactor."

"Is it safe to keep the waste on-site?" I ask.

"We keep the storage as safe as possible," Ted says. "Large cooling ponds hold the used fuel rods. The pools are made of steel-lined concrete. They hold huge amounts of water. The water shields the radioactivity. These ponds

Many people had mixed feelings about nuclear waste at Yucca Mountain. President Barack Obama stopped the project in 2009.

are located in protected places. The waste can be moved to containers for dry storage after enough time has passed."

Ted tells me the dangerous waste created by fission is one of the biggest drawbacks to nuclear power. Geologists have tested different materials to store the waste. They have checked out many possible disposal sites. They have thought about placing waste into the oceans. They have looked into disposing the waste at the places where the ocean and continental plates meet. Some scientists have even looked at shipping the waste to the sun.

RECYCLING NUCLEAR WASTE

Not all used fuel rods are stored in storage ponds. After being reprocessed, the waste can be used again as fuel. Some countries recycle this used fuel. But reprocessing plants are expensive to build. Many people don't want a plant that processes dangerous radiation next door to their homes. Still, uranium is a nonrenewable resource. Once it's gone, it's gone. Reprocessing can reuse as much as 97 percent of the used fuel, helping our uranium supply last longer. The United Kingdom and France are two countries that currently recycle nuclear waste in reprocessing plants.

La Hague nuclear fuel reprocessing plant in Normandy, France, recycles nuclear fuel.

Ted continues, "Researchers decided that the best method was deep underground storage. Other ways proved too risky. Scientists began exploring the Yucca Mountain site by digging a tunnel. But problems came up. Many people in Nevada objected to having the waste stored so close to their homes. And to be stored in Nevada, the waste would have to be moved to Nevada. Many people across the country didn't want nuclear waste traveling past their homes. In 2009, the U.S. Department of Energy decided against building a nuclear waste storage site at Yucca Mountain. They left only the 5-mile (8-km) exploration tunnel."

"Will waste storage continue at reactor sites?" I ask.

"For now—or until there's a place for storage that everyone agrees on."

"Are there any new plans for nuclear power?" I ask.

"Probably!" Ted says. "The newest reactor was built in Tennessee in 1996. But more reactors are in the works. There's a possibility of building mini reactors too. These have a core about the size of a hot tub. Mini reactors would supply energy for about 20,000 homes. Their small size would make them easy to move. They could provide energy in locations where a large, expensive nuclear plant wouldn't make sense."

I thank Ted before heading out. Now that I've learned a little more about the dangers of radiation, I'm curious about how nuclear plants operate safely. ★

March 30: NUCLEAR SAFETY

To learn more about the safety of nuclear plants, I decide to meet with Isabel Santino. Isabel is a Nuclear Regulatory Commission (NRC) safety inspection specialist.

"The NRC sets standards for all nuclear materials," Isabel begins. "The NRC is also responsible for regulating anything related to nuclear energy, fuel, and waste."

Engineers and inspectors make sure nuclear power plants are operating as safely as possible.

PREVENTING TERRORIST ATTACKS

On September 11, 2001, terrorists attacked the World Trade Center towers in New York City. After the attacks, the NRC ordered nuclear power plants to improve security against possible future attacks. The NRC also reviewed security plans of reactors and containment buildings. Experts found that reactors and used fuel pools were designed to withstand most attacks.

Isabel explains that inspectors regularly check reactors, materials, and waste. They test the area around nuclear sites for any problems or radioactivity. The inspectors also check the storage containers, cooling pools, and waste at the reactors.

"Nuclear plants are designed to be as safe as possible," Isabel says. "All plants have built-in safety measures. If an accident occurs, the reactors shut down. People are evacuated. We've worked with people in every field to keep the best technology operating safely."

Isabel pauses for a second. "Despite all these safety measures, accidents still happen from time to time," she says. "Accidents can make people think twice about whether we should use nuclear energy."

Isabel has given me plenty to think about. The NRC takes many safety precautions, but if they fail, nuclear power can be very dangerous. ★

Accidents at nuclear plants can release dangerous radiation into the environment.

April 4:
FUKUSHIMA, JAPAN

My last stop is the nuclear plant in Fukushima, Japan. After a 2011 earthquake and tsunami, Fukushima was the site of a major nuclear accident. I'm ready to learn more about what can happen when there is a problem at a nuclear power plant. Today, I'm on a tour led by Taka Hirano, an officer with the Japan Atomic Energy Agency (JAEA). On the bus ride to the plant, I listen to Mr. Hirano explain what happened in two other nuclear disasters.

The Three Mile Island nuclear plant was the site of an accident in 1979.

"In 1979, there was an accident at the Three Mile Island nuclear plant in Pennsylvania," he says. "That accident didn't kill anyone. But it made scientists take a closer look at nuclear energy. In 1986, Chernobyl, Ukraine, had an even worse nuclear accident. The accident released radiation into the atmosphere. It killed 30 people right away. Later, even more people died from the radiation."

Mr. Hirano explains that most reactors in the United States and other countries have a different, safer design than the one at Chernobyl. Still, the Chernobyl accident led to stricter rules about nuclear power around the world.

He tells us the Fukushima accident in 2011 was different than the other accidents. Fukushima's accident was caused by a natural disaster. He explains that after the earthquake, the plant's safety systems worked at first. The government evacuated people in a 1.9-mile (3-km) radius. But then the tsunami hit. The safety systems failed.

Mr. Hirano explains that the tsunami created a state of emergency. No one could enter the nuclear plant to make repairs. Engineers sampled the seawater for radiation. Workers checked the electrical equipment as soon as they could return to the site. They restored some power. But radiation levels remained high.

LESSONS FROM JAPAN

Nuclear energy continues to play a large part in the U.S. energy plan. Scientists have learned important lessons from the major nuclear disasters. After Japan's 2011 accident, U.S. nuclear plants immediately began working to improve their safety. The NRC made plans for responding to natural disasters, such as earthquakes or tsunamis. They will use what they've learned to improve our nuclear energy production and safety as nuclear energy moves forward in the United States and around the world.

He continues, "We discovered radiation in milk and spinach from nearby areas. It is still uncertain if fish off the Fukushima coast are safe to eat. Many people were evacuated and had to leave their homes. The loss of the power the plant provided means less electricity for the area."

Mr. Hirano adds, "People have strong feelings against nuclear power here in Japan. Some countries, such as Germany and Austria, have decided not to use nuclear power. Other countries, such as South Korea and China, continue to build new plants. Each country must decide for itself if it wants to use nuclear power."

A boy near Fukushima gets checked for radiation.

I've learned so much about nuclear energy. I know no energy source is perfect. Just like any other energy source, nuclear power has its pros and cons. ★

MISSION ACCOMPLISHED!

Great job! You've learned a lot about nuclear energy. You know that nuclear energy comes from a chain reaction caused by splitting atoms. The energy released from the split, known as fission, heats water to create steam. This steam is used to generate electricity. Many people work to keep nuclear energy safe for use. You've seen the problems that can arise from storing nuclear waste. You've also learned about the consequences of nuclear accidents. Nuclear energy can create large amounts of power, but we must find ways to use it safely. Congratulations on a mission well done!

CONSIDER THIS

- Explain how fission can be used to create electricity.
- What safety precautions do nuclear power plants take?
- Describe three nuclear accidents and what scientists have learned from them.

* Why was the Yucca Mountain nuclear waste storage site shut down?
* Explain some of the pros and cons of nuclear power.

Do you think the benefits of nuclear energy outweigh the risks?

GLOSSARY

atom (AT-uhm) the smallest particle of an element

carbon dioxide (kahr-buhn dye-AHK-side) a gas released by the burning of fossil fuels

core (KOR) the inner part of a nuclear reactor

fission (FISH-uhn) splitting an atom to create energy

fossil fuel (FAH-suhl fyoo-uhl) coal, oil, or natural gas formed from ancient plants and animals

nonrenewable (nahn-ri-NOO-uh-buhl) when something cannot be replaced once it is used up

nucleus (NOO-klee-uhs) the center of an atom, made of protons and neutrons

radiation (ray-dee-AY-shuhn) the energy given off during the splitting of atoms

reactor (ree-AK-tur) the structure where atoms are split to produce energy

turbine (TUR-buhn) a machine that spins an electric generator

uranium (yu-RAY-nee-uhm) an element that is used to produce nuclear energy

LEARN MORE

BOOKS

Raum, Elizabeth. *Nuclear Energy*. Chicago: Heinemann Library, 2008.

Reynoldson, Fiona. *Understanding Nuclear Power*. New York: Gareth Stevens, 2011.

Richards, Julie. *Nuclear Energy*. Tarrytown, NY: Marshall Cavendish, 2011.

WEB SITES

Energy Kids

http://www.eia.gov/kids

This site includes history, conversions, and general information about energy.

Kids and Energy

http://www.kids.esdb.bg/uranium.html

Learn more about fission, nuclear power plants, and different kinds of nuclear reactors.

Kid's Korner

http://www.fplsafetyworld.com/?ver=kkblue&utilid=fplforkids&id=16205

Learn more about the discovery of fission and the history of nuclear power.

FURTHER MISSIONS

CARBON SHRINKAGE

The amount of carbon dioxide your actions produce is sometimes called your carbon footprint. Visit an online carbon footprint calculator to estimate how much carbon dioxide your household produces in a year. Examine your results. Where can you reduce emissions? Can you hang laundry in the sun instead of running the clothes dryer? What about growing your own food to reduce driving to the grocery store? What are other things you could do to reduce emissions?

BECOME A NUCLEAR HISTORIAN

Investigate the beginning of nuclear power. Use this knowledge to learn how early discoveries of radioactivity led to Albert Einstein's theory of relativity and the use of nuclear energy in weapons. Start with the origins of nuclear power and how the transition from its use in weapons to energy production happened.

INDEX

ABOUT THE AUTHOR

Shirley Duke is a former science teacher whose love of nature translated into writing for children. She's the author of 17 books for children, most of which are nonfiction. She and her husband divide their time between Garland, Texas, and the Jemez Mountains of New Mexico.

ABOUT THE CONSULTANTS

Mikael Nilsson is an assistant professor of chemical engineering and materials science at the University of California-Irvine. His research specializes in treatment of waste from nuclear power plants. He teaches classes in nuclear chemistry, nuclear fuel cycles, and the handling and practical use of radioactive materials.

Marla Conn is a reading/literacy specialist and an educational consultant. Her specialized consulting work consists of assigning guided reading levels to trade books, writing and developing user guides and lesson plans, and correlating books to curriculum and national standards.